Patchez
Reads About
Endangered
Animals

by Ed Perez
illustrated by Jim Kersell

Cover photos by Corel Corporation.
Photographs on p. 9 by Dominique Braud/Tom Stack & Associates (Left), Thomas Kitchin/Tom Stack & Associates (Right); p. 10 by Gerald Corsi/Tom Stack & Associates; p. 11 by Chip & Jill Isenhart/Tom Stack & Associates; p. 12 by Jeff Foott/Tom Stack & Associates; p. 15 by Gerald Corsi/Tom Stack & Associates (Top), Nancy Adams/Tom Stack & Associates (Bottom Right); p. 17 by Warren & Genny Garst/Tom Stack & Associates; p. 18 by Brian Parker/Tom Stack & Associates (Top Right), Dave B. Fleetham/Tom Stack & Associates (Bottom); p. 19 by Brian Parker/Tom Stack & Associates; p. 20 by Dave Watts/Tom Stack & Associates; p. 21 by John Cancalosi/Tom Stack & Associates; p. 22 by Warren Garst/Tom Stack & Associates; p. 24 by Joe McDonald/Tom Stack & Associates; p. 25 by Gary Milburn/Tom Stack & Associates; p. 26 by Bob McKeever/Tom Stack & Associates; p. 28 by Thomas Kitchin/Tom Stack & Associates; p. 29 by Don & Pat Valenti/Tom Stack & Associates (Top Left), W. Perry Conway/Tom Stack & Associates (Top Right), Jeff Foott/Tom Stack & Associates (Bottom).

≶PAGES℠

Published by Willowisp Press
801 94th Avenue North, St. Petersburg, Florida 33702

Cover design copyright © 1996 by Willowisp Press,
a division of PAGES, Inc.

Printed in the United States of America

2 4 6 8 10 9 7 5 3 1

ISBN 0-87406-824-X

Did you know?

With the tip of its trunk, an elephant can pick up a small coin.

Elephants eat so much that they need many miles of land to find food. And much of their African habitat has become farms and ranches for people.

Another big danger for elephants is *poachers*—people who illegally kill and capture animals. Poachers kill elephants to make jewelry from their ivory tusks.

West Indian Manatee

Manatees are sometimes called "sea cows" because they look fat and eat grassy water plants. Their closest relative is actually the elephant.

To keep warm, manatees live in shallow water along tropical coasts and in tropical rivers. Most stay in the Southern United States, in the state of Florida. They swim very slowly near the surface and are often killed by speeding boats.

Did you know?

Ancient sailors sometimes mistook manatees for mermaids.

Blue Whale

Blue whales are the largest animals on earth. They find their food in the cold waters near the North and South Poles. They travel many miles to the warm waters near the *equator* to have their babies.

For hundreds of years, blue whales have been hunted for their meat and oil. At one time, they were almost extinct. Today, the number of blue whales is growing because people are more aware of the need to protect them.

Black Rhinoceros

The black rhinoceros of Africa can weigh as much as a small truck. It has two horns on its forehead, and when angry it will even attack a train!

The black rhinoceros is in trouble today mostly because of poachers. Poachers kill rhinos, then sell their horns to people who think the horns have magical powers.

Did you know?

Rhinos don't see very well. Sometimes they charge at people—or trees—just to get a better look.

Mountain Gorilla

Mountain gorillas live high in the mountain rain forests of Africa. They don't eat meat but love vegetables. Wild celery is one of their favorite foods. Gorillas live mostly on the ground. Only the young climb trees to play.

The mountain gorilla is one of the most endangered animals in the world. Poachers hunt gorillas for their fur.

Gorillas are a lot like people. They like to take naps at noon. They yawn, sniffle, cough, and even get hiccups.

Green Turtle

Green turtles used to be found in many oceans of the world. But in recent years they have become hunted for their meat and beautiful shells.

Poachers often snatch green turtle eggs from beaches where they are laid to hatch. Many turtles are accidentally killed when trapped in fishing nets.

Did you know?

The green turtle is the only sea turtle that comes ashore to sunbathe!

Florida Panther

At one time, Florida panthers roamed across much of the southern United States. Today, they live only in the *Florida Everglades*. The panther needs miles of land to hunt, but much of its habitat has been turned into farms and cities.

Florida panthers are also in danger from cars. Sometimes, they get run over when they cross highways in search of food.

Did you know?

Tunnels have been built under a Florida highway called Alligator Alley to help panthers cross safely.

Did you know?

    Besides howling, wolves "talk" to each other by the
way they hold their ears, tails and noses.

Gray Wolf

Many people are afraid of wolves, maybe because they howl at night. Gray wolves are *predators*, which means they hunt other animals for food.

At one time gray wolves lived all over the world in cold places. Some still live in tiny areas of North America and Western Europe. Gray wolves are often shot because people are afraid of them and because they attack sheep.

Giant Panda

Many people think pandas are bears. But they aren't. Scientists say the panda's closest relative is the raccoon, a common animal in North America.

Giant pandas live only in far-away bamboo forests in Western China and Tibet. Their main food is tender bamboo leaves. But they are running out of bamboo. Bamboo forests die naturally every 40 years. Some bamboo forests are cleared for farms.

Did you know?

Giant pandas are late sleepers. They are often still resting at nine o'clock in the morning.

Endangered Birds

You might think that because birds can fly anywhere, they would not be endangered. But that isn't true. Sometimes, chemicals used to help grow crops and kill insects accidentally poison the rivers and lakes that birds use.

Other times, the marshy lands some birds live on are drained to make way for new cities and farms.

BALD EAGLE

BROWN PELICAN

CALIFORNIA CONDOR

WHOOPING CRANE

Did you know?

There are dozens of endangered birds. Three of the largest are the California condor, the brown pelican and the whooping crane. All of them can be found in North America. The pelican can also be found in the West Indies and parts of South America.

Helping Animals Stay Alive

The government has passed a lot of laws to protect endangered animals. The bald eagle was once highly endangered, but now its numbers are growing because of strict laws. One law that helped protect it was the banning of a chemical called DDT.

Besides laws, animals can be protected by making sure they have the kind of land they need. Special land that is set aside to help protect animals is called *critical habitat*. National parks often have critical habitats for endangered animals.

Most scientists now think that saving endangered animals one at a time is too hard. Whole areas that contain many kinds of plants and animals—called *ecosystems*—must be protected.

READ **WRITE** **TALK**

What Can You Do?

Talking about endangered animals at school helps make people aware of the problem. Also, writing letters to lawmakers and government officials helps.

Some magazines about endangered animals are just for kids. The magazines *In Your Backyard* and *Ranger Rick* are published by The National Wildlife Federation, 1400 16th Street N.W., Washington, D.C. 20036.

Kids and teachers can also write for information to the United States Department of Interior's Fish and Wildlife Service, Office of Extension Education, 1849 "C" St. N.W., in Washington, D.C. 20240.

You can study how animals live and survive on your own, too. Count the different kinds of birds in your back yard. Watch the insects in your family garden. Visit your local zoo and ask questions. Then share what you learn with friends, family and schoolmates.

Glossary

critical habitat: important land set aside for animals to live.

ecosystem: an area of land where a variety of plants and animals depend on each other for food and shelter.

endangered: when animals are in danger of disappearing forever.

equator: the warmest area of the earth, closest to the sun. The equator is equal in distance from the cold South and North Poles.

extinct: something that no longer exists.

Florida Everglades: a large area of marshy land in the southern part of the state of Florida in the United States.

habitat: where an animal lives.

marsupial: an animal that carries its babies in a pouch on its body.

nocturnal: describes animals that sleep during the day and roam at night.

poachers: hunters who go against the law to kill and capture animals.

predator: an animal that hunts other animals.

savanna: open, level ground with few trees.

Index